THE
CELTS

HAZEL MARY MARTELL

HAMLYN

Acknowledgements

The publishers would like to thank Mrs M. Fry at Historic Scotland, and Nick Brannon and
Anne Hamlin at the Department of the Environment for Northern Ireland, for their assistance in the
preparation of this book; Bill Le Fever, who illustrated the see-through pages; and the organizations
which have given their permission to reproduce the following pictures:

Archiv für Kunst und Geschichte/Eric Lessing: 4-5, 5 top, 9 centre bottom, 12-13.
Ancient Art and Architecture Collection: 24 top, 27 bottom right, 34 top, 45 top right,
/Ronald Sheridan 10 top, 11 top, 13 bottom, /Brian Wilson 9 top right.
Bibliothèque Nationale: 34 bottom, 38 top left. **Bridgeman Art Library/British Museum:** 20 top left.
British Museum: 15 top, 18 top left. **C.M. Dixon/Photo Resources:** 23 top right.
Explorer/A. Le Toquin: 27 centre right. **Historisches Museum Basel/M. Babey:** 29 bottom right.
Historic Scotland: 32. **Simon James:** 23 bottom left. **Life File/Tony Abbott:** 14 top.
The Menil Collection /Hickey-Robertson: 27 centre left.
Moravske Zemske Muzeum: 27 bottom centre. **Musée d'art et d'histoire, Geneva:** 31 bottom right.
Museum Carolino Augusteum, Salzburg: 12 top. **National Museum of Ireland:** 21 centre.
National Museums of Scotland: 45 bottom right. **National Museum of Wales:** 28 top left.
Photographie Giraudon/Chatilloon-sur-Seine, Mus. Archeologique: 21 bottom right,
/Musée des Antiquites Nationales, Saint Germain en Laye 9 centre top,
/Rueil-Malmaison, Mus. Nat. de Château de Malmaison 43 top right.
RCS Libri & Grandi Opere Spa/Muzeul National de Istorie a Romaneiei: 37 top left.
Réunion des Musées Nationaux/Musée des Antiquites Nationales: 19 top right, 27 top.
Scala/Rheinisches Landesmuseum, Bonn: 7 bottom, /Museo del Terme, Rome 39 right.
Society of Antiquaries of London/Geremy Butler: 5 bottom right.
Ville de Beaune, Conservation des Musées/Musée du Vin de Bourgogne/M. Couval: 23 top left.
Werner Forman Archive/British Museum: 8 bottom right, 9 top left, 13 top right,
35 bottom, 37 top right, /National Museum of Ireland 31 top right,
/National Museum of Wales 27 bottom left.
Württembergisches Landesmuseum: 25 top.

Illustrators
Richard Berridge: 28, 29, 30-31, 36, 37.
Peter Bull: 7, 29, 38.
James Field: cover, 42, 44, 45, 46-47.
Ray Grinaway: 8, 9, 10, 11, 20, 21, 43.
Bill Le Fever: heading icons, 16-17, 24-25, 32-33, 40-41.
Tony Randall: 12, 13, 14, 15.
Mark Stacey: 4, 6, 18, 19, 34, 35.
Simon Williams: 22, 23, 26, 38-39.

Editors: Andrew Farrow and Sue Reid
Designer: Mark Summersby
Production Controller: Linda Spillane
Picture Researcher: Liz Fowler

First published in Great Britain 1995
by Hamlyn Children's Books,
an imprint of Reed Children's Books,
Michelin House, 81 Fulham Road, London SW3 6RB,
and Auckland, Melbourne, Singapore and Toronto.

ISBN 0 600 58414 3

A CIP catalogue record for this book is available at the British Library.

Books printed and bound by Proost, Belgium

CONTENTS

THE FIRST CELTS

Early Celtic traders leave their homes near Hallstatt to go to Greece. As well as their goods, they took blankets and hunting equipment as they had to sleep in the open and catch any food they needed.

Long ago, before Rome became a power in the ancient world, the people we call the Celts dominated much of Europe. Their influence ranged from Britain and Ireland in the north to France and Spain in the south and east as far as the Balkans and Turkey. They were united not by a common ruler but by a common language and culture. Though it is now many centuries since their power declined, the influence of the Celtic culture and language remains.

'Almost all the Gauls are of tall stature, fair and ruddy, terrible for the fierceness of their eyes, fond of quarrelling and of overbearing insolence.'
— *Ammianus Marcellinus* —

EARLY TRADERS

The Celts first appear in history in central Europe in the 8th century BC. Some of them crossed the Alps from Hallstatt in what is now Austria to trade with the Ancient Greeks. The Greeks called them Keltoi. This word was probably based on the name the Celts used to describe themselves, as the Romans also called them Celtae or Gauls, but we cannot be certain as the Celts at this time left no written records.

ABOUT THE CELTS

However, scholars from Greece, and later from Rome, left descriptions of the Celts and of how they lived, which we can still read today. Both the Greeks and Romans thought the Celts were uncivilized. This was because the Celtic way of life was so different from their own. The Romans often referred to them as barbarians, and believed them to be a war-loving people who indulged in grisly human sacrifices. They were determined to conquer them and make their lands part of the Roman Empire.

ARCHAEOLOGICAL EVIDENCE

More recently, we have been able to build a different picture of the Celts, based on the work of archaeologists. By excavating Celtic sites and studying the artefacts they left behind, archaeologists now know that the Celts were successful farmers and traders, as well as fierce warriors. As this book will show, they were skilled at making cloth and at mining and working with metals to make tools, weapons, jewellery and ornaments. Unusually for the time in which they lived, they cared for the sick and poor members of their tribes. They were also great story-tellers. They learned their legends by heart and passed them down from one generation to the next by word of mouth.

This bronze container, in the form of a wheeled vehicle and two birds, was made in the 7th century BC. About 18 centimetres long, it probably held food or drink. It was found near Sarajevo, in the former Yugoslavia.

HISTORY AND PREHISTORY

The times before people started writing a record of events are known as prehistory. It is very difficult to fit an accurate time-scale to this period, but in the 19th century archaeologists tried to do this by dividing prehistory into three Ages. These were based on the materials people used for their most important tools and so there was a Stone Age, a Bronze Age and an Iron Age. Because the Celts used iron for most of their tools and weapons, they belong to the Iron Age. The Iron Age itself has now been divided into two periods, based on two collections of Celtic artefacts excavated from sites at Hallstatt in Austria and La Tène in Switzerland.

HALLSTATT AND LA TÈNE

Hallstatt was the older of the two sites and most of the artefacts found there dated from between the 7th and 5th centuries BC. They were excavated from over one thousand graves belonging to people who had become wealthy through mining and trading salt. The site of La Tène on the shores of Lake Neuchâtel was probably occupied from the middle of the 5th century BC until the local Celts were conquered by the Romans. This is the period when Celtic culture was at its peak and it is the time we will look at most closely in this book.

Although iron is a much stronger metal than bronze, it is not as easy to work with. Therefore the Celts continued to use bronze to make fine objects such as this stand which was found in a grave at Hallstatt.

Between 1846 and 1863 archaeologists excavated a cemetery at Hallstatt which contained over 1,000 graves. They recorded their findings in detailed water-colour paintings.

CELTIC EXPANSION

T he iron tools used by the Celts were stronger than the earlier wooden and stone tools had been. This enabled the Celts to clear more land for farming than any of the peoples who had lived in central Europe before them. As they could bring greater areas under cultivation, there was more food for people to eat and the population began to increase. This led to overcrowding, and so some families were forced to find somewhere else to live.

It must have taken migrating Celts a long time to prepare for their journey. As well as household goods and food, they needed tools for farming and building, and seeds from which they could grow new crops.

THE FIRST MIGRATIONS

The early Celts at first looked for land to farm along the fertile valleys of the rivers Danube and Rhine. From there they spread out north, east and west and by the 6th century BC they had started to colonize the lands we now call France, Belgium and Spain. Other Celts had braved the English Channel and settled in the British Isles. Celtic tribes also crossed the Alps and settled in the valley of the River Po in northern Italy.

We can only guess at the difficulties faced by these early travellers. They would have been laden with their possessions, and hampered by their livestock. They had no maps to guide them, no knowledge of the lands they travelled through, and they would almost certainly have met with resistance from their new neighbours!

This map shows the earliest
Celtic settlements of Hallstatt
and La Tène, some of the many
Celtic tribes, and the areas they
moved out to over the centuries.
Celtic expansion was only
stopped when they met enemies
who were more powerful than
themselves.

EXPANSION IN THE EAST

As you can see from the map, however,
the Celtic population continued to expand.
By 358 BC some of the Celts were living as
far east as the Carpathian mountains and
50 years later others had settled in
Moravia. In 278 BC, 20,000 Celtic families
went to Asia Minor to assist Nicomedes,
the ruler of Bithynia, in his fight against
the Syrians. These Celts were known as
the Galatians. When the fighting was over,
they settled in the region which is now part
of Turkey and is still known as Galatia. In
277 BC around 4,000 Celtic mercenaries
travelled to Egypt to fight for the pharaoh,
Ptolemy II. It seems probable that some of
them made their homes in Egypt, too.

CLASHES WITH ROME

At about the same time as the
Celts were spreading out to
the south of the Alps the
Roman Republic was
growing more powerful.
However, the Romans and the
Celts could not live at peace with
each other. Around 390 BC their
armies fought at a place called
Allia and the Romans were
utterly defeated. The
victorious Celts then
marched on to Rome
and plundered and
looted the city.

AN END TO EXPANSION

By around 300 BC the Romans had grown
powerful enough to prevent the Celts
from expanding their Italian territory any
further south. The Celts were also being
resisted elsewhere. In the winter of 279 BC,
Celts and Greeks confronted each other
at the sacred site of the Oracle at Delphi.
With the help of bad weather and
landslides, the Greeks defeated the Celts
and forced them to retreat from Greece
as well.

THE DECLINE OF THE CELTS

Celtic power probably reached its peak
in the 2nd century BC. By that time,
however, other peoples were becoming
more powerful and were threatening the
Celts on three frontiers. In the north they
were harassed by the German tribes and
in the east they were attacked by the
Dacians. From the south the Roman
legions marched relentlessly
onwards. By the 1st century AD,
only Britain and Ireland would
remain as truly Celtic
countries.

We know a lot about what the
Celts looked like from Roman
statues like this one, called the
Dying Gaul. In spite of its
title, it shows one of the Celts
who settled in Galatia.

A wealthy Celtic couple dressed for a feast. The woman is fastening the man's cloak with a brooch. Called a penannular brooch, its pin went through the material, then the top was twisted round to hold it in place.

The Celts wore clothes to keep themselves warm, rather than to be fashionable. This meant that their style of dress did not alter very much from earliest times until after they had been conquered by the Romans. In spite of this, however, we know that the Celts were proud of their appearance. According to the Greek geographer Strabo, they tried not to become fat or pot-bellied as fines were levied on those who became too rotund to do up their belts!

CLOTHING

Men dressed in long woollen trousers, called *bracae*, and wore shoes or ankle boots made from soft leather. When the weather was warm enough, they wore close-fitting sleeveless shirts, fastened at the front with brooches or clasps. When it was cold, however, they wore long-sleeved woollen tunics which were pulled in at the waist with a belt. In really cold weather, they also wore heavy woollen cloaks.

Celtic women dressed simply in long, loose-fitting gowns made from woollen cloth. These were gathered at the waist with a belt, which was usually made from cloth or leather and fastened with a buckle. They draped shawls around their shoulders in cool weather but wore cloaks when it was very cold. Like the men, they usually wore shoes made from leather. Some women must have either worn sandals or gone barefoot, as toe-rings have been found on some skeletons.

Celts checked their appearance in bronze mirrors like this one found in England. The back is richly engraved with a pattern that was probably drawn with a compass. The other side is smooth and highly polished to give a clear reflection.

JEWELLERY

There were no zips or buttons in Celtic times, so the Celts used pins and brooches to fasten their clothing. The most common brooches were called fibulae and were shaped rather like a modern safety pin. Some were quite plain; others were made of gold or silver and might be decorated with coral or enamel. The Celts loved finery and both men and women adorned themselves with bracelets and rings. Women also wore glass or metal beads around their necks.

MEN'S HAIRSTYLES

We know from a Greek writer, Diodorus Siculus, that Celtic men were particular about their hair. They had razors for shaving and used rather clumsy, shearlike scissors to trim their moustaches, of which they were very proud.

> **'Some of them shave the beard, but others let it grow a little; and the nobles shave their cheeks, but they let the moustache grow until it covers the mouth.'**
>
> —— *Diodorus Siculus* ——

Celtic men preferred to have fair hair. If a Celtic man was born with dark hair, he might wash it in limewater to lighten it. Some Celtic men also used limewater to stiffen their hair until it stood up in tufts. Doubtless, this would have added to their frightening appearance in battle!

NEW CLOTHES

Unlike us, the Celts could not go to the shops when they wanted new clothes. Instead, they had to make their own. They also had to make their own cloth, by shearing the wool from their sheep and spinning it into yarn, using a spindle and whorl. To achieve the bright colours and striped and checked fabrics they liked, the yarn was dyed using vegetable dyes from plants such as woad, madder and weld.

WORKING THE LOOM

The yarn was then woven into cloth by the women on an upright loom with a wooden frame. As they had to 'throw' (weave) the shuttle from one side of the loom to the other by hand, the width of their cloth was no wider than their arms could reach. They could weave to whatever length they needed, however, before taking the cloth from the loom. They would then cut it out and sew it with a bone needle.

The Celts used bronze fibulae like the one above to fasten their shirts and tunics and a penannular brooch (top right) to fasten their cloaks. Chieftains often wore heavy bronze armlets; this one from Scotland (top left) is decorated with enamel and coloured glass.

A Celtic moustache and a torque (neck-ring) show up well on this carving found in the Czech Republic. The man is probably a noble.

Spinning and weaving were time-consuming activities. Women probably spent some time doing both every day. If the weather was fine, they worked outside where it was easier to see what they were doing.

SOCIETY AND GOVERNMENT

A gold torque worn around his neck showed that a man was a warrior or a noble.

Learned men were often asked to settle tribal disputes. However, as the Celts were very warlike, some disputes were settled by a fight to the death.

Although the Celts dominated much of Europe, they never had an empire and were never all ruled by one person. Instead, they were divided up into different tribes in different areas. Each tribe had its own leader. Often several tribes would join together to fight against a common enemy, but they were equally likely to fight amongst themselves.

SOCIAL GROUPS

In spite of this, all the Celtic tribes were organized along similar lines no matter where they lived. Celtic society was divided into four main groups: nobles, warriors, farmers and learned men.

RULERS

At the top of society were the rulers, who came from either the noble or the warrior class. They might have inherited their title from their fathers, but in some tribes rulers were nominated by a council of nobles. A ruler's hold on power would probably have been precarious, and often challenged by ambitious noblemen.

Celtic rulers were usually men, but women were also important. Some noblewomen became leaders of their tribes and even went to war! For example, at the time of the Roman conquest of Britain, the Brigantes tribe in the north of England was ruled by a queen called Cartimandua, while in AD 60 Boadicea, or Boudicca, became queen of the Iceni tribe in eastern England after the death of her husband.

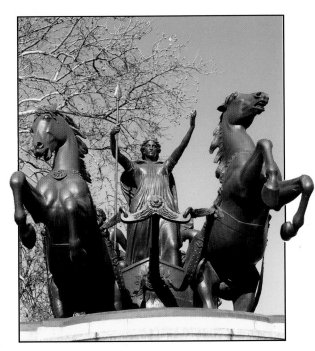

This 19th century statue of Queen Boadicea in her war chariot stands beside the River Thames in London.

LOOKING AFTER THE SICK

The Celts were superstitious and probably believed that sickness was a punishment from their gods. Sometimes they made sacrifices to placate the gods and to assist the patient's recovery. However, in spite of this belief, the Celts tried their best to treat diseases and injuries themselves. Doctors prepared medicines and ointments from herbs and some performed operations. These might include resetting broken bones or even boring into a patient's skull to relieve pressure on the brain after an injury. Unfortunately, as there were no painkillers or antiseptics other than alcohol, few patients would have survived such an operation. As early as 300 BC some of the tribes in Ireland ran hospitals where the old and the sick could be looked after.

The Celts suffered injuries in accidents as well as in battle. This man is being tended by a learned man who is skilled in healing. The man's head wound was probably caused by a fall.

FARMERS AND LEARNED MEN

Farmers made up the largest group in Celtic society, as nearly everybody needed to farm some land in order to eat. Many farmers were also part-time warriors, while the wealthiest among them might also be nobles. Learned men probably did some farming, too, but most of their time would be taken up with other work. They might be doctors, Druids (holy men), metal-workers, or bards or poets. A tribe's bard or poet would have the job of learning their tribe's history and passing it on to the next generation. Learned men were probably also responsible for the smooth running of their tribe.

A CARING SOCIETY

In spite of their love of war and fighting, the Celts lived in a society which cared about the old and the infirm. People who were too old or too ill to look after themselves were usually looked after by younger members of their families. If they had no relations, however, then they were looked after within the local community. Neighbours and friends made sure that they had enough food and heat, as well as adequate clothes and shelter, to make them as comfortable as possible.

MINING AND METALWORK

Celts who mined for salt used tools made from stone, wood or bronze (above) as the salt they were digging out would have rusted iron tools away. There was no explosive gas in salt mines, so they could use a naked flame for light. Even so, conditions must have been dark, cramped and miserable.

The Celts owed a lot of their wealth to two related skills. These were mining and metal-working, in both of which they excelled. As well as mining metals, they also mined for salt.

MINING FOR SALT

Celtic farmers could never grow enough fodder to feed all their farm animals over the winter. Because of this, at the end of the autumn they slaughtered those animals that were not needed for breeding the following year. The meat was then used to feed the farmer and his family throughout the winter.

As there were no refrigerators or deep-freezers, the only way to stop their meat from going bad was to preserve it with salt. People who lived near the coast could obtain their salt quite easily by collecting sea water in salt-pans and letting it evaporate until only salt crystals remained.

For people living inland, this was much more difficult. However, in the mountains around Hallstatt there was good quality salt underground. The miners had to make sloping shafts in the mountainside. Next they dug tunnels into the salt using picks. It was a difficult and very dangerous job. Despite this, the Celts of Hallstatt were able to mine enough salt to supply all their own needs and still have enough to trade with their neighbours.

MINING FOR COPPER

The Celts in central Europe also mined for copper ore. This could be smelted and turned into metal quite easily. However, copper on its own is quite soft, so it is usually mixed with tin to make an alloy called bronze. In early Celtic times, most bronze tools and weapons had been replaced by stronger iron ones, so bronze was used mainly to decorate weapons and to make jewellery and household utensils.

The Gundestrup cauldron from Denmark is a fine example of Celtic metal-working skills. It is made in silver and gilt and embossed (moulded) with figures both inside and out.

BRONZE

By Celtic times, bronzesmiths knew how to cast molten bronze into ingots which could be hammered into bronze sheets of various thicknesses. They also knew how to cast bronze into moulds made from stone, clay or bone, to make all sorts of small objects.

DIGGING FOR IRON

The iron from which the Celts made tools and weapons comes from iron ore. Iron ore was more plentiful than copper ore and was also much easier for the Celts to obtain. It was often found in nodules, or lumps, in marshy or wooded areas. This meant it could be dug out of the ground without using complicated mining techniques. The iron ore was then placed in a small, bowl-shaped furnace. This relied on the wind to provide enough draught to make the charcoal fire burn hot enough to smelt the ore. When it was hot enough, a bloom, or lump, of purer iron formed in the bottom of the furnace.

As well as tools and weapons, Celtic blacksmiths made ornamental items for the homes of the wealthy. This one is making a firedog, which is a stout framework in which a fire can be contained. The piece on the anvil would be finished off in the shape of an animal's head.

THE BLACKSMITH'S FORGE

Iron was more difficult to work with than bronze, because it would not melt properly at the temperatures the Celts could achieve in their simple furnaces. The bloom of iron that was smelted out of the ore was too stiff to pour into moulds. In order to make objects from it, it had to be forged by the blacksmith. To do this, he held the bloom of iron in long-handled tongs over his fire until the iron glowed red-hot. He then started to hammer it on his anvil into the shape he wanted. Once the iron began to cool, the smith stopped hammering and held it back over the fire until it was red-hot again. He could then carry on shaping it until it cooled down again. He repeated this process until he had completed the object.

The Celts were both creative and practical people. The bronze design on this iron spearhead is just for decoration, but the bronze bands on the wooden bucket (below) are more practical, as they hold the wooden staves together and stop the bucket leaking.

DAILY LIFE

In Spain the Celts built many of their houses with stone walls, so the remains of some of them can still be seen today. These ones are at Castro de Coaña in Asturias. As you can see, they are round in shape and stood near the top of a hill.

Daily life for most Celts centred around the home. At first, most lived in isolated farmsteads with their families. However, Celts who had become rich through trading in goods such as salt and iron built themselves forts to protect their wealth. In later times, communities grew up which developed into fortified towns and villages.

HILLFORTS

The Celts built their forts on the top of hills, which not only made them easy to defend, but also gave them a good view of the surrounding countryside. The earliest Celtic hillforts date from between 800 and 600 BC and are found in the area immediately north of the Alps. By 600 BC hillforts were being built in what is now eastern France and south-west Germany.

In Britain, there had been hillforts as early as 1000 BC, before the arrival of the Celts. Both then and in early Celtic times hillforts seem to have served a different purpose from many of those in mainland Europe. Instead of being the homes of wealthy traders or princes, they were first of all places where a local tribe could gather in times of danger. Later, some of the hillforts might have housed religious centres, where the tribe could meet for ceremonies, before developing into the fortified villages. It must have taken the Celts months to build the protective banks that surrounded their settlements, as all the soil had to be dug out with shovels and piled up without the help of any machinery.

OPPIDA

The settlements known as 'oppida' were the Celtic equivalent of our towns and villages. Most of them were market centres. Although some of them were surrounded by earthworks, they were not as well defended as the hillforts. Some oppida developed into important trading centres. By the 1st century BC, many of them had paved roads and drainage systems, probably copied from Roman towns that Celtic traders had visited.

Although this settlement is small, it is defended by ditches and banks, topped by a sturdy fence. The only way in and out was through the gates where an enemy could easily be seen and defeated. In peaceful times, the fence also kept the farm animals in - or out.

14

THE FAMILY

An oppidum might have contained any number of houses. These were occupied not just by a man, his wife and children, but by a large extended family. This could include any of the man's unmarried brothers or sisters until they got homes and families of their own. Elderly parents might also live with one of their married children, as might any unmarried uncles or aunts. Members of the family were very supportive of each other and put kinship ties above loyalty to their tribe.

HOUSEWORK

The Celts did not have any labour-saving devices, so a lot of their time was taken up with keeping the family fed and clothed. Much of this work was done by the women, but the men probably helped too when they were not too busy with the farmwork. One job which had to be done frequently was grinding grain into flour to make bread. This had to be done by hand on a stone quern. In the earliest of these, the grain was placed on a large, flat stone and ground into flour by rubbing a smaller stone backwards and forwards over it. Using this method, it could take an hour and a half to produce just one kilogram of flour! After the 2nd century BC, however, the invention of the rotary quern speeded this job up and a kilogram of flour could be produced in 10 minutes.

CHILDREN

There were no schools in Celtic times so children were at home all day. They probably learned to do things by watching their parents and other family members until they were old enough to help with simple jobs in the house and on the farm. These might include picking weeds out from the crops and scaring the birds away, or helping to comb the tangles out of the wool before it was spun into yarn. Celtic children probably also found time to play, probably with simple dolls and models of animals.

Games of chance seem to have been popular as coloured glass counters have been found at some excavations. Sadly no sets of rules exist now, so we do not know how the games were played.

In this scene inside a Celtic house, the woman on the right is using a rotary quern to grind grain into flour, while the woman on the left is shaping dough into loaves. These would then be baked in the beehive-shaped oven in the background or on a heated stone slab on the hearth.

15

HOUSE AND HOME

In the see-through scene below we can see buildings in a Celtic settlement, perhaps in Gaul (France). Some of the villagers are building a new grain store, on the left - perhaps rain has been seeping into the grain pit and making the grain go mouldy. In the pool (bottom right), some villagers are mixing mud or clay to daub on the grain store's wattle panels.

Celtic family homes in Britain, Spain and Portugal were often round in shape, but in other parts of Europe they were usually square or oblong. Most of them had a steeply sloping roof of straw or reeds. This was so that rain or snow would run off quickly, rather than soaking through and causing the roof to collapse. The walls were built with whatever materials were available locally. In some areas stone was used, but wood was more usual. This might be made into wooden planks, or a wooden frame to support wattle-and-daub.

INSIDE THE HOUSE

Celtic houses had just one big room in which everybody ate, slept, cooked and did their daily chores. There was probably very little furniture as the ancient writers tell us that the Celts sat on animal skins. These were either spread out on the floor, which was made of hard-packed earth, or on a bench built along the wall where people slept at night. The hearth with its fire was the most important feature of a Celtic home. It provided heat for cooking and also gave off light. This was essential as the houses had no windows. The fire also made the house dirty, however, as there were no chimneys and soot often fell inside if the smoke could not escape through gaps in the thatch.

OUTBUILDINGS

As well as building a house for themselves, some Celts built a shelter for the animals and a store for the hay which they fed them on. They probably also had a shelter for their plough, their tools and any farm carts or chariots they owned. They also had special buildings in which grain could be stored in sacks for a short period. Unlike the other buildings, these had a wood-planked floor and were raised above the ground on legs to prevent rats and mice getting in and eating the grain. The Celts also kept some of their grain in storage pits. These were about 1.8 metres deep and were lined with wicker or stone. Once they were filled with grain, the pits were sealed with clay to keep the air out.

1 Timber frame
2 Wattle-and-daub walls
3 Thatched roof
4 Hearth
5 Packed earth sleeping platform
6 Grain store

HARD WORK

The Celts had no power tools to help them, so building a house must have been very hard work. The right sort of timber had to be cut down in the forest and brought back to the site. It was then trimmed into shape ready to make the frame. Holes were dug for the upright posts, and the main timbers were strapped into position. Meanwhile, reeds or straw had been cut and dried for the thatched roof. The walls were filled in with wattle-and-daub panels. These were made by weaving together long thin twigs and plastering them with thick mud.

Twenty years later, the house would probably have to be rebuilt as all the materials would be rotting.

7   Constructing a grain store
8   Grain storage pit
9   Protective earth rampart
    and ditch
10 Wooden palisade

Celtic houses had thick thatched roofs to keep out the rain and the wind. They do not seem to have had smoke-holes or chimneys, but perhaps the smoke slowly worked its way through the woven reeds. You can lift the see-through page to see inside the house. There are very few furnishings - just a hearth and a raised platform for sleeping on.

FOOD AND FARMING

A Celtic farmer's tools, such as these sheep-shears and sickle, were very much like those still used by farmers at the start of the 20th century.

Farming was very important to the Celts, no matter where they lived. This was because there were no food shops, so each family had to grow all its own food. This would have been difficult work, as Celtic farmers did not have the many aids such as chemical fertilizers and machinery which we take for granted today.

PLOUGHING THE FIELDS

Like all their other farming tools, the Celts' plough was better than any that had been used before in central and northern Europe. Although it was still made mostly from wood, it had an iron tip which not only made the plough stronger, but also could be replaced easily. Celtic ploughs could not turn the soil or dig very deep, however, so they were only useful where the soil was light and easy to work.

Because of this, Celtic farmers preferred to farm in upland areas, rather than in the valley bottoms where the soil was heavier. To break up the soil more thoroughly, the fields were probably ploughed twice, the second time at a right-angle to the first. Stones were pulled out and thrown to the side, where they eventually formed boundaries between fields. These can still be seen today in parts of Britain and Ireland.

CROPS

Just like farmers today, the Celts grew grain crops such as rye, wheat, barley and oats. They also grew vegetables such as beans and lentils which could be stored over the winter and eaten when other food was scarce. Some fields were also used as pastures or for growing grass. This was cut in the summer and dried to make hay to feed any livestock kept over the winter.

At least two people were needed to plough a field: one to guide the ox team and the other to guide the plough. Other people were kept busy picking out the stones the plough turned up and driving the cattle away from the newly-ploughed area.

SEED, BREAD AND BEER

In Celtic times crops did not produce as many seeds or grains as their equivalents do now, so quite large amounts had to be harvested to provide all of a family's needs. The whole family probably helped with the harvesting. The crops were then taken back to the farm buildings to be threshed by hand. This removed the chaff (husks) and left a pile of grain.

Some of the grain had to be saved as seed for planting the next year's crop. The rest of it was stored in grain pits until it was needed (see page 17) . Most of the stored grain would be ground into flour for bread or meal for porridge and stews, but some of it was used to brew beer.

FARM ANIMALS

As well as growing crops, the Celts kept animals on their farms. These were early breeds of the animals you would expect to see on farms today. They included pigs which were kept for their meat, cattle which provided meat, milk and leather, and sheep which provided milk and wool. As sheep were kept primarily for their wool, they were not killed until they were old - by which time their meat would be too tough to eat. Hens and geese too were kept, for their eggs and feathers, but it was against the law to eat their flesh. The Celts probably also kept swarms of bees in wickerwork hives to provide them with honey, which was the only sweetener available in ancient times.

HUNTING

The Celts also enjoyed hunting the fierce animals which roamed the woods and forests surrounding their farms. Their favourite was the wild boar which they liked to eat, but they also hunted wolves and other animals which might eat their flocks and crops. They usually killed the animals with long-handled spears but sometimes they used iron-tipped arrows or even sling-shots.

As you can see from this bronze model from Spain, the Celts rode on horseback when they went hunting. The bell on the horse's neck would perhaps frighten the boar out of hiding and the dog would chase it until it was tired and easier to catch.

Old grain pits were filled in with rubbish. This often included items such as cracked pots and broken tools which provide archaeologists with valuable evidence of Celtic life. In the background some men are unloading freshly-cut timber.

FEASTS AND CELEBRATIONS

Decorated flagons, like this one found in France, were used to serve wine at a rich man's feast.

Feasts and celebrations were the highlights of the Celtic year. They were usually rowdy, often extravagant affairs at which the Celts could indulge their love of eating and drinking. At large feasts the whole tribe could meet together to display their unity and loyalty to their chieftain. Some feasts were held to celebrate special festivals in the Celtic year, such as the New Year. Others were held just to bring people together, rather as we might throw a party for no particular reason today.

SPECIAL FOOD AND DRINK

Alcohol played an important part at feasts. Wine was brought from Italy for those who could afford it, but poorer people drank beer brewed from wheat and perhaps sweetened with honey. Sometimes the drink was served in a cup which a slave or young boy carried from one person to the next. The men were said to drink only a little at a time from this cup, but they were also said to do it frequently and were well-known for their drunkenness!

As well as drinking a lot, the Celts enjoyed eating meat at their feasts. This would either be roasted on a spit or stewed in a huge cauldron with herbs and vegetables. There might be pork, beef, wild boar and anything else the hunters had caught. The bravest warrior expected the best cut of meat and might start a fight if he didn't get it.

Celtic feasts were colourful, as well as noisy, with everyone wearing their best clothes and jewellery. At this one the bard is telling a story, while a man in the background is playing music on a flute. The person on the left is serving wine imported from the Romans.

The priests or Druids probably played a large part in all the Celtic festivals. At Beltane they supervised the building of the bonfires and the driving of the cattle between them.

HOSPITABLE HOSTS

The Celts were hospitable and often welcomed strangers to their feasts. The writer Diodorus Siculus reported, 'They also invite strangers to their banquets, and only after the meal do they ask who they are and of what they stand in need.' As well as being plied with food and drink, guests would be entertained by the tribe's bard with stories of the tribe's past glories. Boasting contests might also develop between warriors eager to tell of their prowess in hunting and battle.

SAMHAIN

Samhain was the name for the Celtic New Year and was the most important of the Celtic festivals. It was celebrated on 1 November when the animals were brought in from grazing and those not needed for breeding were slaughtered for food. Because Samhain belonged neither to the old nor the new year, it was also thought to be a time of magic, when armies of magical soldiers marched out from caves and mounds in the earth, and people and spirits could mingle in each other's worlds. In Christian times, Samhain was replaced by All Saints' Day or All Hallows' Day. The day before it became known as Hallowe'en. Some of the old Celtic beliefs still linger in traditional Hallowe'en celebrations.

The harsh cry of Celtic trumpets and great horns probably announced the beginning of ceremonies and festivals. This war trumpet comes from Ireland.

BELTANE

Beltane was celebrated at the beginning of May and was the second most important day in the Celtic year. It marked the time when the cattle were sent out to graze in the open again after being sheltered and fed near the farmhouse all winter. As part of the celebrations, the Celts lit huge bonfires and drove their cattle between them. It was believed that this would protect the cattle from diseases.

IMBOLC AND LUGNASAD

These festivals were celebrated by many of the Celts, but they were not as important as Samhain or Beltane. Imbolc, on 1 February, was celebrated as the start of the lambing season when the ewes' milk was plentiful again. This was important not only for feeding the lambs, but also for making cheese. Lugnasad, on 1 August, was celebrated as the time when the crops began to ripen in the fields, giving the promise of a good harvest and plenty to eat over the coming winter.

This cauldron, called a krater, would be filled with wine at a feast. It was made of bronze and would hold many litres!

The Celts had many gods and goddesses. Some were worshipped by all Celts, while many tribes had their own special gods. There were gods of warfare and hunting, and goddesses of fertility, healing and good harvests.

GODS OF NATURE

The Celts were mainly farmers who relied heavily on the seasons and the forces of nature for their survival, so their religion was closely related to their natural surroundings. Many of their gods and goddesses were associated with trees, stones, lakes and springs. Each tribe also had its own tribal god.

Over all of these deities reigned the Earth Mother. It was believed that all gods and goddesses demanded respect, and so offerings and sacrifices were sometimes made to them.

To make sacrifices to their gods, the priests threw valuable items such as gold cups and weapons into the water. The blades of swords, knives and daggers were often bent over or broken before they were thrown in.

HOLY WELLS AND SPRINGS

The Celts relied on natural wells and springs as a source of drinking water for themselves and their animals. Because water came from the earth, it was associated with the Earth Mother, so most of the wells and springs were thought to be the homes of goddesses, rather than gods.

One of the most important of these goddesses was Elen, who was also a goddess of healing. Another was Sulis who guarded the hot springs at Bath. When the Romans later built a town on the site, they named it after her, calling it Aquae Sulis, meaning 'Waters of Sulis'. The Celts believed that the water goddesses had the power to make sick people well, to protect people in battle or to prevent a particular spring from drying up in a drought. If a Celt wanted to ask a favour of a water goddess, he might make a sacrifice to her by throwing some of his most valued possessions into the water.

SACRED GROVES

Certain groves of trees were as sacred to the Celts as churches or temples are to us. According to the Roman poet Lucan, the Celts let the sacred groves grow wild so that the branches of the trees met over-head and blocked out the sunlight. Within these groves, there were images of the gods which were roughly carved from tree-trunks. There were also altars on which the Druids, or priests, performed sacrifices. These might have been animal or even human sacrifices, as Lucan said the trees were sprinkled with human blood.

THE DRUIDS

Religious ceremonies and sacrifices were performed by the tribe's priests. In Britain and Gaul the priests were known as Druids and probably came from noble families. The Druids were also teachers and versed in the laws of the tribe. Sometimes they even made decisions about whether the tribe should go to war or not. Many of their rituals were performed in secret. They never wrote anything down and they also forbade other people to read or write. Their knowledge was passed down by word of mouth and it could take up to 20 years for a novice to acquire all the knowledge he needed to become a Druid.

One of a priest's tasks was probably to put together a calendar for the year. This one, found in France, shows lucky and unlucky days.

OAK TREES AND MISTLETOE

To the Celts, the oak was the most sacred tree. Mistletoe was thought to be sacred too and was believed to aid healing and encourage fertility.

'They believe that the mistletoe, taken in drink, imparts fertility to barren animals, and that it is an antidote for all poisons.'

— Pliny —

However, as the juice of mistletoe was drunk by sacrificial victims it seems likely that the Druids were also aware of its poisonous properties!

Many carvings and statues of Celtic gods have been found. Above you can see three different images of the water goddess Coventina. The statue on the left is of the Dagda, or Good God, of Ireland.

Only Druids were allowed to enter the sacred groves where the mistletoe grew. They cut it with a golden sickle and caught it on a white cloth so that it did not touch the ground.

PRINCELY TOMBS

The early Celts believed that there was a life after death. They thought that when a person died, he or she went to a place known as the Otherworld where life went on much the same as before. After a time, a person would die in the Otherworld and be reborn in this one. This meant that people might be reunited with their families and friends time after time.

When you turn over the see-through page you will see inside the tomb of a noblewoman found beneath a stone cairn at Vix in France. She had been placed on a wagon, along with pottery such as this decorated cup from Greece (right). On the right you can also see part of the decorated rim of the huge Greek bronze krater, or cauldron, that was buried with her.

GRAVE GOODS

The Celts often buried some of a dead person's favourite belongings with the body. These might be their best clothes and other objects that would be useful in the next world. The Celts also buried things which the person might need on the journey to the Otherworld, such as food and drink. Joints of pork were a firm favourite, and one man was buried with 40 litres of Italian wine!

1 Noblewoman wearing torque
2 Wagon
3 Wheels from wagon
4 The Vix krater
5 The Hochdorf prince
6 Bronze couch
7 Drinking horns
8 Bronze dishes on wagon
9 Bronze cauldron from Italy
10 Flowers

CREMATIONS

Some Celts also cremated their dead, rather than just burying the bodies. After the cremation, the remains of the bones were put into a pot or an urn and this was buried in a small grave. Even this burial, however, often contained food and drink and other items that might be useful in the Otherworld. In some regions very few Celtic burials have been found - perhaps in these regions the Celts simply scattered the ashes of their dead.

CHARIOT BURIALS

Chariots were as important to the Celts in death as they were in life. As well as probably transporting the dead person to his grave, a chariot was often also buried with him. It might be taken to pieces and the wheels laid on their sides in the bottom of the grave with the body on top of them, or it might be left standing upright and in one piece.

No one is sure whether these chariots were supposed to take the dead person on the journey to the Otherworld or whether they were a mark of a person's high standing in this one. In one case two horses were buried as well!

PRINCELY TOMBS

This name is given to many spectacular graves found mainly in parts of Germany and France. As you can see from the picture below, they appear from the outside as a large grassy mound sticking up in the landscape. Unfortunately, because this made them so visible, they later became easy targets for grave-robbers who stole much of the gold and other treasures which had been buried with the dead.

The scene below shows early Celts building a mound, or tumulus, over the tomb of a prince. The Hochdorf prince, who is shown under the see-through page, was buried beneath a mound like this.

Turn over the see-through page below to see inside the tomb of a Celtic prince. He was buried in about 525 BC at Hochdorf in what is now Germany. His wooden burial chamber was built in a pit, then a mound over six metres high and 60 metres in diameter was piled above him. On the left is one of the bronze lions that decorate a huge cauldron found in his tomb. When you lift the see-through scene you will see that the prince must have been wearing shoes decorated with gold when he was buried, as these gold bands were found on his feet.

25

CRAFTWORKERS

Just as they were able to produce their own food and make their own clothes, so most Celtic families were also able to make the utensils and simple tools they needed for their daily life. If a Celt wanted something special, however, and could afford it, he would visit a craftworker who made a living from producing fine objects.

AMAZING ARTISTRY

The artistry of Celtic craftsmen was renowned in the ancient world. But when archaeologists first discovered beautifully-made objects on Celtic sites, they thought the Celts must have imported them from other peoples such as the Greeks or the Romans. They could not believe that the Celts had the skills needed to produce such fine workmanship in glass, enamel, gold and bronze, as well as in silver, iron and wood. But gradually archaeologists began to find evidence, such as special moulds, tools and waste products, which showed that the Celts had indeed made many of the things themselves.

THE GOLDSMITH

Gold was the Celts' favourite metal for jewellery and decoration. To make jewellery such as the torques, or neck-rings, the goldsmith first stretched out the gold to make thin strands of wire. These were then twisted together into what looked like a golden rope. This was bent into shape to fit around the warrior's neck and the two ends were completed with an ornamental end of gold, called a finial. These were often patterned by being formed in a decorated mould.

However, if the goldsmith wanted to decorate an object such as a special pair of shoes, he would first shape the gold into small bars, or ingots. These were then hammered out into a large, flat sheet which could be cut out into a delicate pattern or stamped with a patterned die.

Many of the Celts' favourite designs were based on circles. A pair of iron compasses was used to scratch the outline of the design onto the metal of the object to be decorated. The shapes could then be cut out to make an openwork pattern or filled in with coloured enamel.

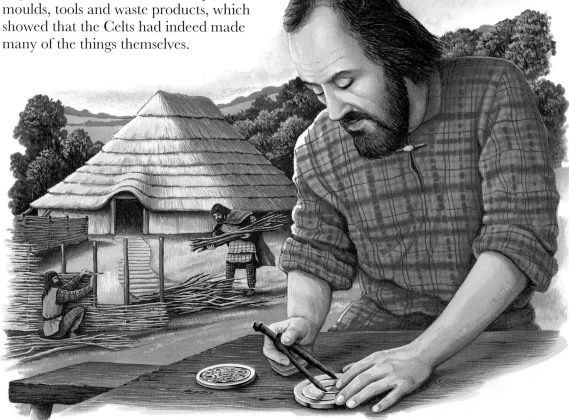

GLASSWARE

By about 250 BC the Celts in central Europe had discovered how to make glass. They could only make it in very small amounts, however, and so could not use it for anything useful such as windows for their houses. Instead, they used it to make ornaments and jewellery such as beads and bracelets. The Celts were particularly fond of coloured glass. They produced different colours by adding different minerals, such as powdered copper and iron, to the glass while it was still molten or liquid. Once a bead or a bracelet had been made, patterns could be added to it by trailing small amounts of different-coloured liquid glass onto it. Some patterns were also moulded on while the bracelets and beads were being made.

WORKING WITH ENAMEL

The Celts liked to decorate their bronzeware with enamel. This was usually coloured bright red, which was the Celts' favourite colour, but yellow, blue and green enamels were also popular. To make the enamel, Celtic enamellers heated a mixture of quartz glass, lead ore and a mineral such as cuprite at a high temperature in a stone or clay crucible. The enameller then got the object he wanted to decorate and roughened the surfaces which were to be enamelled. Next he poured the hot liquid enamel on to the object. As it cooled, it stuck firmly to the roughened surfaces. If more than one colour of enamel was wanted on a particular object, the enameller needed a very steady hand to make sure the second colour went into the right part of the pattern!

CELTIC DESIGN

Some of the distinctive designs on our jewellery today were originally created by Celtic craftsmen. Many of these designs were based on circles, which Celtic craftsmen made with iron compasses. Swirling patterns and the three-legged triskele, which is still used today as the emblem of the Isle of Man, were also popular. Another favourite was the animal motif. From the number of glass and metal animals that have been found, we know that animal ornaments were popular.

Here are some of the items made by Celtic craftworkers. Most of them are made from bronze and decorated with enamel or with delicate filigree patterns, but the helmet also contains some silver and is decorated with coral.

The glass flask (right) from Germany was made in about AD 250, but the glass beads on the necklace and bracelet (below) are from the 4th century BC.

27

TRADE

Iron bars like these have been found on Celtic sites. About 80 centimetres long, they were probably used as currency, but could also be used to repair iron tools and weapons.

From the earliest times, the Celts traded with each other and with their neighbours. They travelled long distances to exchange any surplus goods or raw materials for those that they could not produce themselves. Because their civilization lasted for so many centuries and covered such a wide area, the Celts' trading partners included the Phoenicians and the Carthaginians, as well as the Etruscans, the Greeks and the Romans. These peoples also traded with other peoples, so that the Celts could obtain items from all parts of the ancient world, even from countries as far away as China.

SALT, TIN AND COPPER

The earliest recorded Celtic traders were those tribesmen who took salt over the Alps from their mines around Hallstatt to the cities of Greece. There must have been traders before these, however, as tin and copper - the two metals which are needed to make bronze - were not found in all parts of Europe. Copper was the more widely available, but tin was only found in what are now Cornwall, Brittany and north-west Spain and Portugal. This meant that to reach bronzesmiths in other parts of Europe, traders had to transport the tin long distances overland. They might even have had to cross the sea.

BARTER OR CASH?

For many centuries, the Celts bartered for the goods they wanted rather than paying for them with money. They also paid for goods by giving the seller their value in iron bars. In later Celtic times, however, coins came into widespread use, so the Celts were able to pay for goods with them. The first coins used by the Celts were brought from Greece by Celtic mercenary soldiers.

LUXURY GOODS

Although the Celts were able to produce beautiful objects themselves, rich Celts imported luxury goods to enhance their status in the community. At first these goods were laboriously carried over the mountains by Celtic traders. By about 600 BC, however, the Greeks had established a trading colony, called Massilia, near the mouth of the River Rhône. Massilia gave Celtic traders access by sea to other Mediterranean ports and along the river valleys to most of the western Celtic lands.

This made the transport of goods much easier. Many of the luxurious objects that have been found in Celtic burial grounds in France, Germany and Switzerland must have travelled along these routes.

Slaves who had been captured by the Celts were sold to the Romans in exchange for goods such as wine. They often ended up in the slave markets of Rome. There they were sold to the highest bidder who might well have then taken them to work in an entirely different part of the Roman Empire.

As this map of their trading routes shows, the Celts transported their goods both by land and by sea. Not all the Celts made long journeys, however. Instead, they might take their goods to one place and exchange goods with a trader from another place, then both parties would return home.

TRADE WITH THE ROMANS

The Celts' most important trading partners were the Romans, especially as the Roman Empire increased in size. To run this empire successfully, the Romans relied heavily on slave labour. Slaves did not just serve in the houses of the rich. They were put to work on farms and in mines and other industries. Some slaves were people who had been captured by the Celts and traded to the Romans, often in exchange for fine Italian wine. The Romans felt they were getting the better bargain, as the Celts would accept just one jar of wine for a slave.

The Romans were especially fond of the woollen cloth produced by the Celts. They probably used the checked and striped designs for blankets, but their favourite was plain red cloth from the Celts in Britain.

However, what seemed like folly to the Romans was not necessarily prompted by an excessive love of drink! In Celtic society, the possessor of such fine wine was held in high esteem.

CLOTH AND POTTERY

As well as buying slaves, the Romans bought good quality woollen cloth from the Celts. Though some Romans mocked the Celts as barbarians who dressed in animal skins, in fact their cloth was of far better quality than anything the Romans could produce. In exchange, the Celts took Roman pottery and glassware. A lot of the pottery was bought by the Celts in southern Gaul. They made cheap imitations of it and in turn traded these with other Celts who lived further north.

This pottery from Italy, together with fragments of amphorae (jars) which had contained wine, was found at the site of a Celtic trading settlement on the River Rhine in Basle, Switzerland.

TRANSPORT

Though travel in Celtic times was much more difficult than it is today, the Celts successfully transported themselves and their goods around much of Europe and the Mediterranean. Sometimes they had to go on foot, but they also travelled by horse, by chariot and by cart, depending on the sort of terrain they were travelling over. The Celts were also skilled boatbuilders, so those Celtic tribes who lived by the water were able to travel by boat.

DANGEROUS JOURNEYS

The Europe inhabited by the first Celts was much more heavily forested than it is today. This made it difficult to get about and quite a few early travellers must have got lost and died of hunger or exhaustion. Some might also have been attacked and killed by the wild animals which roamed the countryside in large numbers. Travellers in the high mountains would also have had to cope with the bitter coldness, as there were few places for them to shelter. Many of them must have died on the journey.

WHEELED TRANSPORT

In regions where the ground was not too rough, the Celts often travelled by four-wheeled carts or wagons. Like their chariots, wagons had wooden wheels with iron tyres. They were pulled by two horses which were harnessed to a wooden yoke, fixed to a central pole. As a horse uses its chest muscles when pulling a load, however, this method would not have been very comfortable for the horse, nor would it have been very efficient. Though the wagons were useful for families on the move, there were not many smooth roads in the Celtic lands, so they were probably only used over short distances.

A trading vessel has arrived in the Celtic port of Geneva. Some Celts in coracles are helping to unload the goods, which others will take away on carts or in smaller boats. Archaeologists have discovered the remains of a 30-metre-long pier and wooden palisades which protected the port from wind and waves.

TRAVELLING ON WATER

Many Celts lived alongside rivers or lakes, so boats were important for getting around as well as for going fishing. The simplest of these were coracles which can still sometimes be seen today in parts of Wales. These were usually circular, but were sometimes shaped like an oblong with rounded corners. They were made of a wickerwork frame with waterproofed animal skins stretched over it and sewn together. They carried one person who paddled with a single oar. Because they were very light, coracles could easily be lifted out of the water and carried around any obstacles, such as rapids or waterfalls.

The Celts used coracles on rivers and lakes and for short sea journeys. For longer sea journeys, however, the Celts had bigger boats which were made from wood. These could have several pairs of oars and also had a mast so that they could be sailed as well as rowed, depending on conditions on the sea at the time.

SEA JOURNEYS

Travelling by sea was probably even more dangerous for the Celts than travelling into the mountains. They had no charts or maps and had to rely on the sun and the stars to navigate their way. Even the biggest ships, such as those of the Veneti of western France, could easily be wrecked if a gale blew up suddenly. Because of this, the Celts tried to sail as close to the land as possible and crossed the open sea at its narrowest points.

JOURNEYS IN EASY STAGES

In general the Celts only sailed along parts of the coast which they knew well. When they reached unknown waters they would sail into the nearest harbour and transfer their cargo to another vessel whose crew knew the waters. If the Celts were transporting goods over any long distance by sea, there might be several changes of boat and crew before the cargo reached its final destination.

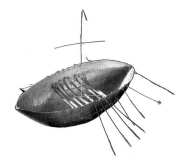

This model of a Celtic ship is made from gold and was found in Ireland. It might have been an offering to Manannan mac Lir, King of the Ocean.

The Celts believed their port of Geneva (in Switzerland) was protected by a god who is shown in this large oak statue, which dates from around 80 BC.

A BROCH

From archaeological evidence we know that most Celtic houses were only one storey high. In about the 1st century BC, however, Celts living on the north coast of the Scottish mainland and in the Northern and Western Isles began to build tall, round structures known as brochs. Built from the local stone, they were between 12 and 25 metres in diameter at the base, but narrower at the top. They were at least 15 metres high and their walls were constructed without using any mortar. Brochs had an inner wall and an outer wall, fastened together in places by long stones. Between the two walls, stone staircases led to the different floors, or galleries.

AROUND A BROCH

On the sites of many brochs the remains of other Celtic buildings have been found. These include the houses where the people normally lived and the buildings in which they sheltered their animals and stored their food. There was often also an outer wall to help defend the whole site from enemies. After the end of the 1st century AD, it seems that the brochs were abandoned and fell into disrepair. However, many sites remained occupied, and the stones from the brochs were used to make new buildings.

The broch in the main scene is based on one at Clickhimin in Scotland. There had been a settlement on the site for many years. Later, a gatehouse was built to guard the entrance. Lift up the see-through page to see the settlement with the broch, and inside the broch.

1 Building guarding outer gateway
2 Double stone wall
3 Staircase
4 Timber gallery
5 Thatched roof
6 Stone hearth
7 Parapet

INSIDE A BROCH

Brochs were built to protect the Celts in times of danger, so the entrance was usually through a single door at ground level. This door led into an open courtyard with a well or hearth in the middle. The living areas were above this on galleries or platforms built out from the inner wall. These galleries had wooden floors and walls. Their roofs sloped down towards the courtyard and were thatched with reeds or straw. More than one family would have sheltered in a broch, so conditions must have been very cramped. It must also have been dark and cold inside, even on a bright day, as the high walls with no windows stopped the sun shining in.

This diagram shows how brochs may have evolved from the drystone ramparts of settlements and forts. People later built ranges of buildings against the ramparts. The tall brochs would have provided better protection from attackers using fire and slingshots.

broch

wall of fort

buildings inside wall

This picture of the ruins of the broch at Dun Carloway on the Isle of Lewis clearly shows the structure of the double walls with the space for the stairs in between. Over 500 brochs were built by the Celts.

Horses were very important to the Celts. They were not only a means of transport but were also ridden for pleasure. There was even a Celtic horse goddess, known as Epona, who was worshipped in Gaul and Britain.

COINS AND CAVALRY

We know that the Celts were very proud of their mounts because horses and chariots are shown on their gold coins from around the 1st century BC. The Romans greatly admired their horsemanship, and recruited many cavalrymen from Celtiberia (Spain) and Gaul into their army.

HORSES AND HARNESSES

Nobody is sure when horses were first ridden in Europe. It is likely that the Celts used them as early as 700 BC, as large numbers of harness fittings have been found from this time. These include bits for the horse's mouth which are similar to those used by riders today. Enamelled harness-mounts, which the Celts used to decorate as well as to strengthen the harness, have also been found. The various leather straps of the harness were linked together by bronze and iron rings. There is no evidence that horses wore shoes, but as the Celts did not ride on paved roads, these were not important.

Chariot racing was one of the Celts' favourite sports. Chariots were not used in battle after about 200 BC, except in Britain, but the nobles continued to travel and race in chariots for many years.

On this statue found in France, the goddess Epona is shown as a woman with a horse.

Archaeologists can learn about Celtic harnesses and chariots by studying coins like this one.

34

SHOWING OFF

Just as some people now take great pride in their cars and want them to look better than anyone else's, so the Celts took pride in the way their horses looked. Gold coins show horses with their manes braided or plaited and there is evidence that some of them wore caps. Pony caps were worn principally to protect the horse's head from injury. However, it is clear from the fine workmanship of many of these caps that they were also worn for decoration. A pony cap found in Scotland was made from bronze and decorated in a raised pattern of swirls and circles. It had a hole at each side through which the pony's ears would fit and possibly a third hole in between them which could have held a feathered plume. On another pony cap, tags of metal were attached to the end of streamers, and these would have jangled as the pony moved.

RACING

The Celts were fine horsemen and charioteers who loved to show off their horsemanship. The big races, which were often part of the entertainment at the great feasts, provided the perfect opportunity for the Celts to show off their skills - and for the spectators to gamble on who would win. It is likely that the races also helped young warriors develop the skills they would later need in battle.

A Celtic raiding party might steal cattle and other valuable goods from their neighbours, as well as from their enemies. Raiding also helped the Celts practise their riding and fighting skills.

THE USE OF CHARIOTS

The chariot was the Celts' favourite vehicle. It was lighter and more mobile than a wagon and could even be used on hunting expeditions where the forests were not too thick. When the Celts were at war, however, the chariot was used in battle. Then it held two men. One was the charioteer who held the reins and steered the horses. The other was a warrior who could fight from inside the chariot, or even standing on the front pole to which the horses were yoked. Mostly, warriors used chariots to take them into battle, then ran down the pole to fight on foot. If the fight went against them, their charioteer collected them and drove them to safety.

MAKING A CHARIOT

Because wood soon rots in the soil, no complete chariots have yet been found. However, we know that they were made of wood and that their wooden wheels had an iron tyre which was fitted whilst it was hot. It would then shrink as it cooled and so hold the parts of wheel firmly together. After the wheels had been made and fixed onto their axle, the flat body of the chariot was made and joined to its pole. Panels of wickerwork were then added to the two sides to protect the people in the chariot, but the front was probably left open to make it easier for the warrior to jump out and fight on the pole in times of battle.

This Celtic horse bit is similar to those used today. The mould used to make the bit, and a guiding ring, are shown above it.

WARRIORS AND WARFARE

The Celts tried to frighten their enemies into running away without a fight. Here, an important Gallic warrior tries to intimidate his Roman enemy by challenging him to single combat. However, Roman soldiers usually stood their ground and were able to defeat the unorganized Celts.

Warriors were very important people within Celtic society. Their courage in battle was highly respected and they often fought in other people's armies as well as for their own tribe. Death held no fear for the Celtic warrior, who could imagine no greater glory than to die in battle. To avoid the dishonour of being taken prisoner, many warriors committed suicide.

WEAPONS

Even the poorest warriors had weapons of some sort. A common weapon was the spear or javelin, which could be up to 2.5 metres long. It had an iron head fixed onto a wooden handle and was probably thrown at the enemy at the start of a battle, rather than used like a lance to stab him. According to Julius Caesar, the Celts in Gaul also had bows and arrows, while on several sites in Britain archaeologists have found piles of small stones which were probably used in sling-shots.

Wealthier warriors also carried swords. In early Celtic times, swords had short blades and were rather like daggers. These would only have been really useful for hand-to-hand fighting. From the 3rd century BC, however, improvements in technology meant that swords could be made much longer. Using these swords to slash at the enemy, warriors could also fight from horseback.

ARMOUR

Many Celtic warriors carried a shield to defend themselves in battle. It was usually made of a flat sheet of wood and was often covered with leather to protect it from heavy blows. In shape it was an oval or a rectangle with rounded ends, and could be up to 1.4 metres tall. The grip or boss in the centre was often made of iron and could be used as a weapon in hand-to-hand fighting if the shield itself was destroyed. Some Celts protected their heads with helmets made of leather, bronze or iron and, from the 3rd century BC, a few warriors also wore chain-mail shirts to protect their bodies. Chain-mail was probably a Celtic invention but, as each shirt took a long time to make and was very expensive, possibly only the most important warriors wore them. In contrast, some Celtic warriors went into battle totally naked, apart from the torques around their necks!

WAR CHARIOTS

The Celts in mainland Europe only used chariots until the 2nd century BC, with the last recorded use of them being at the Battle of Telamon in 225 BC. Even then, they may well have been used simply as a means of getting the warriors quickly into battle and out of it again, with all the fighting being done on foot. In Britain, however, the Celts rode chariots into battle until at least the 1st century AD. As explained on page 35, they were able to fight from the chariots, hurling spears at their enemies as they rushed by them at great speed.

CELTIC CAVALRY

It used to be thought that Celtic warriors could not have fought properly from horseback because they did not have stirrups (foot-rests). Now, however, it has been realized that by the 3rd and 2nd centuries BC the Celts were using a saddle with four tall pommels. These held the rider firmly in his seat and allowed him to use his thighs for balance. This left him his arms free to control his horse and his weapons, with little fear of falling off.

BATTLE TACTICS

Celtic battles seem to have been chaotic affairs. The Celts' armies were often huge, but Celtic soldiers lacked discipline and there were no real battleplans. Instead, the Celts tried to frighten their enemies into giving up without a fight. First, the most important warriors might try to intimidate their enemies by taunting them. As the taunts were accompanied by fierce war-cries and by the harsh din of the battle trumpets, this tactic must sometimes have proved successful! If this failed, however, the Celts charged at the enemy at full speed, brandishing spears and swords. If the enemy stood their ground, Celtic warriors would fight to the death, rather than admit defeat.

A wealthy Celtic warrior would probably have worn a helmet or a shield like these for impressing people at ceremonies, and only at important battles.

The Celts thought the head was the most important part of a person's body. If they got the opportunity, they severed the heads from enemies they had killed and took them as trophies. Here a warrior is showing a head to his allies in Hannibal's Carthaginian army.

THE ROMAN CONQUEST

This gold coin from the 1st century BC shows the head of the Gallic chieftain Vercingetorix. After he surrendered to Julius Caesar at Alesia in 52 BC, he was taken to Rome as a prisoner. In 46 BC Caesar paraded him through the streets of the city, before having him executed.

The Romans' defeat at the Battle of Allia and the sacking of the city of Rome, described on page 7, was a humiliation they had not forgotten. They were determined to crush the Celts and drive them from their lands.

DEFEAT IN ITALY

By 225 BC, with an organized and well-equipped army, the Romans were able to put this plan into action. At the Battle of Telamon the Romans inflicted a massive defeat on their Celtic enemies: 40,000 warriors were killed and at least 10,000 more were taken prisoner. Celtic influence in Italy was destroyed. But such a massive defeat was to have even more serious consequences for the Celts. The Romans realized they could add the Celts' lands to their rapidly growing empire.

This map shows some of the Romans' major victories and conquests in the Celtic lands, and other battles involving the Celts. Many tribes were wiped out completely, but others adopted Roman ways and their warriors often became soldiers in the Roman armies.

ALLIES OF HANNIBAL

The expansionist plans of the Romans were not only a threat to the Celts. Around 218 BC, alarmed by Rome's growing might, the Carthaginians of North Africa formed an alliance with some of the Celtic tribes to make an assault on Rome. Under the leadership of the Carthaginian general, Hannibal, an army set out to march through Spain and Gaul before crossing the Alps into Italy. At the River Ticinus the combined force of Carthaginians and Celts defeated the Romans in battle. But the allies' military success was short-lived. By 202 BC, the Romans had crushed the Carthaginians and increased their own influence in the Mediterranean region.

CONQUESTS IN GAUL

After defeating the Carthaginians, the Romans turned their attention once more to the conquest of the Celtic lands in Europe. Though the Celts resisted bravely, they lacked the discipline of the Roman soldiers. By around 60 BC, Celtic lands in Spain and northern Italy were in Roman hands. Julius Caesar, one of Rome's most brilliant soldiers, was put in charge of the security of two new Roman provinces in northern Italy, Cisalpine and Transalpine Gaul. Caesar was an ambitious man, looking for the chance to gain wealth and glory. He knew that conquering the whole of Gaul (France) would help him achieve his ambitions.

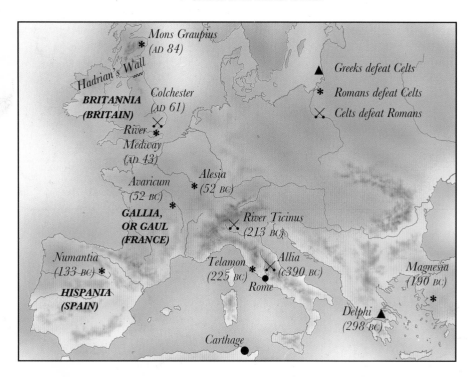

Mons Graupius (AD 84)

Hadrian's Wall

BRITANNIA (BRITAIN)

Colchester (AD 61)

River Medway (AD 43)

Avaricum (52 BC)

Alesia (52 BC)

GALLIA, OR GAUL (FRANCE)

Numantia (133 BC)

HISPANIA (SPAIN)

River Ticinus (213 BC)

Telamon (225 BC)

Allia (c.390 BC)

Rome

Magnesia (190 BC)

Delphi (298 BC)

Carthage

▲ Greeks defeat Celts
✳ Romans defeat Celts
✗ Celts defeat Romans

CAESAR'S TRIUMPH

When Caesar's army marched into Gaul, some Celtic tribes were quick to form alliances with him. Those that resisted, however, were treated with great ruthlessness. The Nervii tribe was almost completely destroyed and the Eburoni tribe was wiped out.

In 52 BC, under the leadership of Vercingetorix, chieftain of the Arverni tribe, the Gallic Celts made a bold attempt to rid their lands of the Roman invaders. Vercingetorix seems to have been a clever and courageous leader, but he was eventually trapped by the wily Caesar when he was forced to retreat to the hilltop oppidum of Alesia. Caesar promptly laid siege. Although a relief force of 250,000 Celts came to the aid of the besieged Celts, Vercingetorix was forced to surrender. It had been the Gallic Celts' last great stand. Now Gaul, too, became part of the Romans' empire.

BRITAIN

The Romans under Caesar made a number of attempts to conquer Britain, but it was not until AD 43, in the reign of the Emperor Claudius, that they were able to bring parts of Britain under Roman rule. Many British Celts resisted the Romans just as bravely as had the Celts on the mainland of Europe, but others forged alliances with them. As in Gaul, this made it easier for the Romans to subdue Celtic resistance. However, conquest of the north and west proved impossible and around AD 120 the Emperor Hadrian built a new northern boundary for the Roman Empire. This boundary became known as Hadrian's Wall. Running from coast to coast, much of it remains today.

Rather than be taken prisoner and perhaps sold into slavery, the Celtic chieftain in this marble statue from Rome has killed his wife and is about to kill himself.

At the Battle of Telamon an army of around 70,000 Celts was trapped between two Roman armies. As well as being better organized, the Romans had superior equipment, and they heavily defeated the Celts.

THE COMING OF CHRISTIANITY

The see-through scene below shows part of a Celtic Christian monastery. Originally all of the buildings were made of wood and wattle-and-daub. By the 10th century the main buildings, such as the church and refectory, would have been rebuilt in stone. If they were attacked by raiders, such as plundering Vikings, the monks could seek refuge in the stone tower.

Christianity was adopted by the Celts during Roman times. A few Celts had learned about the new religion through their trading links with people from around the Mediterranean. The Romans allowed the vanquished Celts to continue worshipping their old gods, but at first tried to forbid Christianity. They thought it threatened their authority and so the first Christians had to keep their religion secret. Those who were discovered were persecuted.

THE FORBIDDEN RELIGION

In spite of this, the number of Christians increased, especially among the poor. Then, in 312, the Emperor Constantine became a Christian after a great victory in battle, and he made Christianity the religion of the Roman Empire. When Germanic tribes destroyed Roman power in western Europe, the Church in Rome sent missionaries to convert their chieftains.

CHRISTIANITY IN BRITAIN

In 410 the Roman legions left Britain and went to defend other parts of their empire. Parts of Britain were also under threat from Angles and Saxons who migrated to the south and east coasts in search of new lands to settle. These people brought their own religions to their new homelands and Christianity became confined to a few people in the Celtic west of the country, which was untouched by the invaders.

SAINT PATRICK

The most famous Celtic Christian was St Patrick. Patrick was born on the west coast of Britain around AD 385. His grandfather was a Christian priest. When he was 16, Patrick was captured by pirates and taken to Ireland. He later escaped to France where he trained to be a Christian priest. Then around 432 he went back to Ireland as a bishop. His first attempts to convert the Irish to Christianity met with great opposition, but eventually he was successful. Patrick also persuaded some of his followers to build monasteries.

1 **Stone church**
2 **Altar**
3 **Wooden look-out tower**
4 **New stone look-out tower**
5 **Monks' dining hall, or refectory**
6 **Souterrain, an underground chamber for storage**
7 **Brackets holding burning rushes**
8 **School, where monks studied**
9 **Abbot's house**
10 **Monk's house, or cell**
11 **Gate-keeper's house**

THE WORK OF THE MONKS

The Christian religion which survived in Ireland and Britain became known as the Celtic Christian Church. By the end of the 5th century, many Celtic Christians had set up monasteries in Wales, Cornwall and Brittany as well as in Ireland.

The monks wanted little to do with politics and worldly affairs. Instead they spent much time praying and studying their Bibles. They also looked after the sick and the poor, supporting themselves by farming. Some of the monks left the monasteries to convert other people to Christianity. Others stayed behind to make beautifully decorated copies of religious books. Some of these, such as the Book of Kells and the Lindisfarne Gospels, can still be seen today.

The Celtic monks lived a simple life, and had very few personal possessions. However, they made and cared for beautiful objects, such as chalices (cups) and books. When the monks copied out manuscripts, they often decorated the pages with designs similar to those used on early Celtic jewellery. As well as putting patterns on the borders of the page, the monks also made the first letter on a page look especially beautiful.

MYTHS AND LEGENDS

A s well as boasting about their personal exploits, Celts loved to tell stories of their tribes, their leaders and their gods. They also liked to invent stories of imaginary heroes and heroines. These were passed from one generation to the next by word of mouth, and many of them must have been lost or forgotten. In Britain and Ireland, however, some of these stories and legends were written down after the decline of the Druids, and can still be read today.

By the 12th century AD the legends of King Arthur had spread as far as Italy, but they still contained some strong Celtic elements. For example, after Arthur had been mortally wounded in battle, he asked one of his knights to return his sword, Excalibur, to the Lady of the Lake, just as the Celts had sacrificed swords in the past.

KING ARTHUR

Probably the most famous stories from Celtic times are those about King Arthur. These stories were first told in the 6th century AD, and were possibly based on the life of a Welsh Celtic chieftain.

The legend of King Arthur became even more popular after the Norman conquest of Britain in 1066, when more stories were added to the old ones. Arthur was then portrayed as a medieval knight and the original story was turned into one of chivalry, courtly manners and romance. Travelling minstrels told the stories throughout Britain, France and even Italy, and in 1165 Arthur was pictured in a mosaic in Otranto in Italy. At about the same time, the great French poet Chrétien de Troyes wrote several romances about the characters of King Arthur's court. Although these stories were very different from the original Celtic ones, they were the ones recorded and illustrated in medieval manuscripts.

THE MABINOGION

The most famous of the Celtic legends from Wales were probably written down in the 11th century, but the stories themselves are much older. There are 11 stories altogether, four of which relate to Pryderi, an early Prince of Dyfed (in Wales). Arthur also appears in these stories, which were given the name *The Mabinogion* in the 19th century.

THE IRISH LEGENDS

Irish literature gives us the largest number of Celtic legends. Many of them were written down by Christian monks, but even so they tell tales of the old Celtic gods and goddesses, as well as of mortal heroes and heroines. They are one of our best sources for finding out how the Celts looked at life, but, like the stories of King Arthur, they are not a true account of Celtic history.

Many of the Irish legends are contained in three sets of stories, or cycles. The first tells of battles between supernatural races who invade Ireland. The second, called the Ulster cycle, describes a hero with magical powers, named Cú Chulainn. Finally, the Fenian or Ossianic cycle tells of another hero, named Finn MacCool, his son Oisin (Ossian), and their band of warriors known as the Fianna, or Fenians.

CELTIC WRITING

Although Celtic monks recorded many of these stories, some of the first things written by the Celts were inscriptions on stones. The letters were made up of straight lines to make them easy to carve into the stone. The letters used on stones in mainland Europe are largely based on the alphabets used by the people the Celts had most contact with. Some of the Celts in Britain developed their own alphabets, however. One alphabet used in Wales was made up of 30 letters, while the Ogham alphabet used in Ireland and western Britain had 25 letters.

This picture of the Irish Celtic hero Ossian was painted in the 19th century. By then his story had changed a lot from the original version. Here he is seen receiving the soul of Napoleon Bonaparte into heaven!

The stone on the left is inscribed with the Ogham alphabet, while the one below shows very early letters that were used by Celts in northern Italy.

After the conquest of the Celtic lands by the Romans, many Celts adopted Roman ways. The Druids were suppressed, and people were encouraged to practise other religions, including those of the Romans and, later, Christianity. Celtic nobles were allowed to become Roman citizens and officers in the army, and some were even made senators. Many Romans left Italy to live in Hispania (Spain) and Gallia (France), which became two of the richest provinces in the Empire.

ROMANIZATION IN THE WEST

On mainland Europe, 'Romanization' was quite thorough. In some of the old Celtic lands, particularly those closest to Rome, Celtic culture disappeared completely. However, in some areas where the Celts had resisted the Roman invasion, the Romans were reluctant to give much power to the local Celts. In these regions the Celts held onto more of their old traditions, and in some places the Celtic way of life went on almost unchanged.

SURVIVAL IN BRITAIN

Though most British Celts also adopted Roman ways, many of the Celtic tribes bitterly opposed Roman rule. Therefore Celtic culture survived more successfully in Britain than on the mainland of Europe. However, even in Britain, the survival of the Celtic way of life was strongest in the places which never became part of the Roman Empire or which were only slightly influenced by the Romans. The most important of these were Ireland, which the Romans never visited, and Scotland, which the Romans were never able to conquer. Wales and Cornwall also remained strongly Celtic, as they were only on the fringe of Roman influence.

In 60 AD, thousands of Celts, led by Boadicea of the Iceni tribe, revolted against Roman rule in Britain. They attacked and burnt the new Roman towns of Colchester, London and St Albans and killed around 70,000 Romans and their supporters, before they themselves were defeated. In Colchester (below), the Roman citizens made a last desperate stand at the Temple of Apollo, a symbol of Roman influence.

The Tara brooch was made in Ireland in the 8th century AD. Its design is still copied today.

THE NEW KINGDOMS

Following the departure of the Romans, chaotic times came to Britain as there was no longer one power in control. The south and east of Britain were invaded by Angles and Saxons, while the Irish Celts invaded the west. These Celts were known as the Scotti and eventually they gave their name to the country we call Scotland. Others settled in Gwynedd and Dyfed (Wales) and from there invaded the regions we now call Cornwall and Devon. In turn, Celts from Cornwall and Devon moved to Gaul and settled in the region called Armorica. They took their language and customs with them and the area eventually developed into an independent state which became known as Brittany.

THE CELTIC LANGUAGES

Although the Celtic languages died out in most of Europe, they survived in Britain, Ireland and Brittany. Most of them have recently undergone a revival as people in Celtic areas have become more aware of the importance of their Celtic inheritance. Erse, Gaelic, Welsh and Breton are still spoken in Ireland, Scotland, Wales and Brittany, while Manx, which was spoken on the Isle of Man, and Cornish, have only recently died out.

The Celts in Ireland were not directly affected by Roman rule, but in the 9th century AD they suffered raids from the Vikings. The Vikings later settled on the coast and set up trading centres at places such as Dublin and Cork. The Vikings often formed alliances with Irish chieftains, who were frequently at war with each other.

PLACE NAMES

Even where Celtic language and culture no longer exist, the names of some towns, cities, regions and even countries remind us of the Celts who once lived there. For example, Paris is named after the Parisii tribe, and Belgium is named after the Belgii. Lyon in France takes its name from Lugh, the Celtic sun god, as does London. In north-west England, the name Cumbria is based on the word Cymry, meaning fellow countrymen, which is what the British Celts called themselves.

Although the Romans overwhelmed the Celts, Celtic influence survives today - not just in place names and art, but in the many people who are descended from the original Celts.

This powder horn was made in Scotland in 1693, but you can see the Celtic influence in the intertwined patterns that have been carved into it.

KEY DATES AND GLOSSARY

Because both the Greeks and the Romans wrote about their encounters with the Celts, we can be sure of the dates of many events from about 300 BC onwards. Before this time, we have to rely on the work of archaeologists. By doing scientific tests on the artefacts they find, they can tell us when the objects were made and this in turn tells us when a site was occupied.

At the hilltop oppidum of Alesia, the Gallic Celts, led by their chieftain Vercingetorix, made a last great stand against the Romans. Here the Celts are being attacked in the rear as they make a desperate attempt to break through the siegeworks built by Julius Caesar's army.

BC

750   By this date Celts are living in the Hallstatt area of Austria and becoming wealthy by trading salt.

500   La Tène civilization begins to develop.

c390   The Celts defeat the Roman army and attack Rome.

298   Celts attack the Oracle at Delphi but are defeated by the Greeks.

278   Around 20,000 Celts fight for Nicomedes of Bithynia against the Syrians. The land they settle in becomes known as Galatia.

225   The Celts suffer a crushing defeat by the Romans at the Battle of Telamon.

224   The Romans invade Cisalpine Gaul.

218   Helped by the Celts, Hannibal's Carthaginian army crosses the Alps to attack the Romans. This begins the Second Punic War.

202   The Romans finally defeat the Carthaginians at the Battle of Zama, ending the Second Punic War.

198   The Romans set out to conquer Gaul.

197   The Romans take control of Spain.

190   The Galatians ally themselves with the Greeks and are defeated by the Romans at the Battle of Magnesia. Later they ally with the Romans.

121   The Romans take control of Transalpine Gaul.

60   The Boii tribe of Bohemia is defeated by the Dacians.

58   The Helvetii leave their homelands and head towards Gaul. Caesar uses this as an excuse to move his army into Gaul.

55   Most of Gaul is under Roman control. Caesar sends an expedition to Britain but is unable to establish Roman rule there.

52   Celtic resistance in Gaul is crushed at the Battle of Alesia. Vercingetorix surrenders, and is beheaded in 46 BC.

AD

43	Roman conquest of Britain begins.
61	Boadicea leads the Iceni tribe in revolt against Roman rule.
74	Galatia becomes part of the Roman province of Cappadocia.
122	Hadrian's Wall marks the north-west limit of Roman expansion.
312	The Roman Emperor Constantine makes Christianity the official religion of the Empire.
410	The last of the Roman legions leave Britain to defend Rome.
450	By this date, Celts from Britain have settled in Brittany.
c793	The Viking raids start.
1014	Irish King Brian Boru defeats the Vikings and their allies at Clontarf.

Glossary

artefact: any object that has been made by a person.

barter: to obtain goods by exchanging them for other goods of a similar or higher value.

fodder: food such as hay which is used to feed animals.

Oracle: one of the most important holy places to the Ancient Greeks.

sack: to rob a town or a city, usually with much violence and destruction.

scabbard: the cover made to fit over the blade of a knife or a sword.

sling-shot: a strap used to hurl stones with great force.

spindle and whorl: a weighted stick used to spin a single thread by hand.

wattle-and-daub: building material made by interweaving thin pieces of wood and filling the gaps with mud or plaster.

Quotations

The Roman Ammianus Marcellinus wrote about the Celts in the 4th century AD when most of the Celtic lands were under Roman rule. Strabo was a Greek geographer who lived from 64 BC to AD 21. As well as living in Rome and Alexandria, he travelled widely and wrote 17 books on geography. Most of his information on the Celts came from the work of an earlier writer called Posidonius. Diodorus Siculus also wrote in Greek and traced the history of the world up to the end of the Gallic wars in a 40-volume work called *Library of History*. He died in 20 BC. Lucan was a Roman poet who was born in Spain in AD 39. His full name was Marcus Annaeus Lucanus and he died in AD 65. Pliny was a Roman scholar and soldier who died in AD 79. His 37-volume work, *Natural History*, gave details of the Druids and of Celtic medicine. Julius Caesar, who died in 44 BC, wrote about the Celts in his work on the Gallic Wars.

INDEX